Entryways and Doorways

Jo Cryder

4880 Lower Valley Road   Atglen, Pennsylvania 19310

EMMA S. CLARK MEMORIAL LIBRARY
Setauket, L.I.; New York 11733

Other Schiffer Books by Jo Cryder
1000 Dormers.
1000 Fences and Gates.
1000 Shutters & Awnings.

Other Schiffer Books on Related Subjects
Architectural Details from Old New England Homes. Stanley Schuler.
Art Nouveau Ironwork of Austria & Hungary. Federico Santi & John Gacher.
Doors of Oaxaca. Devon Fekete.
Doorways of Cape May. Tina Skinner & Melissa Cardona.
Early Domestic Architecture of Pennsylvania. Eleanor Raymond.
Half-Timber Architecture. Tina Skinner.
New England Architecture by Wallace Nutting. Wallace Nutting.
Old World Inspiration for American Architecture. Richard S. Requa.

Copyright © 2008 by Jo Cryder
Library of Congress Control Number: 2007943191

All rights reserved. No part of this work may be reproduced or used in any form or by any means—graphic, electronic, or mechanical, including photocopying or information storage and retrieval systems—without written permission from the publisher.

The scanning, uploading and distribution of this book or any part thereof via the Internet or via any other means without the permission of the publisher is illegal and punishable by law. Please purchase only authorized editions and do not participate in or encourage the electronic piracy of copyrighted materials.

"Schiffer," "Schiffer Publishing Ltd. & Design," and the "Design of pen and ink well" are registered trademarks of Schiffer Publishing Ltd.

Type set in Americana XBd BT/Arrus BT

ISBN: 978-0-7643-2858-9
Printed in China

Schiffer Books are available at special discounts for bulk purchases for sales promotions or premiums. Special editions, including personalized covers, corporate imprints, and excerpts can be created in large quantities for special needs. For more information contact the publisher:

Published by Schiffer Publishing Ltd.
4880 Lower Valley Road
Atglen, PA 19310
Phone: (610) 593-1777; Fax: (610) 593-2002
E-mail: Info@schifferbooks.com

For the largest selection of fine reference books on this and related subjects, please visit our web site at **www.schifferbooks.com**
We are always looking for people to write books on new and related subjects. If you have an idea for a book please contact us at the above address.

This book may be purchased from the publisher.
Include $3.95 for shipping.
Please try your bookstore first.
You may write for a free catalog.

In Europe, Schiffer books are distributed by
Bushwood Books
6 Marksbury Ave.
Kew Gardens
Surrey TW9 4JF England
Phone: 44 (0) 20 8392-8585; Fax: 44 (0) 20 8392-9876
E-mail: info@bushwoodbooks.co.uk
Website: www.bushwoodbooks.co.uk
Free postage in the U.K., Europe; air mail at cost.

Contents

We zoom right in to take a close-up look at front doors to homes. There are twenty styles of doors and their many accents. To further assist you, the chapter has sketches of doors to identify their features followed by tables with page numbers.

In the chapter are pictures of outer doors, such as security doors, storm doors, screen doors, and louver doors that have been installed over the main entry doors. The pictures are broken down into six different categories of outer doors.

The chapter discusses the architectural features of entryway styles. It starts with homes where the main door is flush with the surface of the house and the door stands alone. In this style of entryway there is little or no cover above the door. The entryway styles develop from there to trimmed doors, doors with surrounds, entryways with roofs, recessed doors, different styles of porches, and finally pergolas. There are fourteen different categories of entryway styles.

This chapter presents an assortment of approaches where stairways are used to access the entryway. The stairways might start at the street or sidewalk, the driveway, after a walkway, or from under the house.

Walkways and driveways dress up an entryway as much as landscaping and architectural features.

When you see a term in the text and aren't sure what is meant by it, refer to the Glossary for an explanation. Included in the Glossary are some reference websites.

Introduction

To read "The Symbolism of the Pineapple" by Hoag Levins, go to: www.levins.com/ pineapple.html
Savannah, Georgia

This is my fourth book on architectural elements. All four books have the same presentation style. I have had a chance to see how people approach my books. One of the first comments they make after looking through one of my books is that the places where the pictures were taken seem to be mixed up. I'm bringing this to your attention up front to help you understand that the pictures are not grouped by location. They are grouped by categories and so locations may appear in several categories. The location is given for each picture, but that information is incidental. Seeing the subjects side by side provides an opportunity to compare them to each other as well as to study the content of each picture.

This book is put together to study entryways to homes and will build on the knowledge acquired from each section. For instance, we are going to start with close-ups of door systems. After you've reviewed that information you are going to see and be able to recognize styles of door systems throughout the book. Then we'll review styles of entryways, i.e., doorways, alcoves, porches, etc. That information can be used as you review the entire book. Then we'll cover stairways, walkways, and driveways. A Glossary is provided at the back of the book featuring terms used throughout the text, and their accompanying definitions. Also included in the glossary are some websites where more information can be found.

One thing we all have in common in our houses is exterior entryways. We want them to look their best for ourselves, for visitors, and for when the day arrives when we put the house up for sale.

Approaching a home, the walkway, a stairway, the entryway, and the door can set the stage for what is inside. These stage-setters can be clean and simple, and be totally acceptable. Or they can be enhanced simply or elaborately. Healthy plants and flowers, statuary, welcoming furniture, and fresh appearing paint go a long way to enhancing this whole area. Following those basics, more elaborate entryways expand the possibilities with the amount of effort and money invested in them. But, be aware, too simple may look bare, while too elaborate may appear cluttered and overdone.

An interesting thing for you to do would be to take your own picture of the front of your home and evaluate it the same as you will evaluate the pictures in this book. Check to see how your home compares to homes with similar entryway construction. Refer to the book to get ideas how you can improve what you already have. If you are in the process of designing the remodeling of the entryway or building a new home, these photos can help you plan your interim and final goals.

Chapter I. Doors

Door Styles

Your entryway makes a statement and sets the tone for the rest of the house. The entryway should set the standard for what's to come. The first ingredient in an entryway that we are going to look at is the door—from single doors and twin doors to doors with accents (transoms and sidelights) to doors with glass windows. Some new doors have UV rated insulated glass for energy efficiency, others may have beveled, silk-screened or stained glass with genuine brass caming. Some doors have adjustable blinds assembled inside a double glass pane. There's a wide array of glass: standard or custom etched patterns, double paned, clear or frosted, and tinted.

The sketches at the right and on page 28 will assist you in understanding a variety of door styles that are available, and the order they appear in this chapter.

To locate a certain style of door system, refer to the tables on pages 6 and 29.

Exterior Door Sketches

Doors with Accents

The simple sketches of doors below show the basic variety of configurations for doors. The doors themselves can be plain, paneled, or carved and decorated. Transoms basicly have three distinct shapes; arch, ellipse and box. Sidelights are made in a variety of shapes and sizes. Door hardware is available in a large variety of materials, colors, shapes and sizes.

Single doors that have no glass windows.

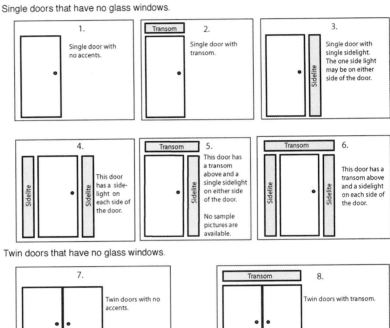

Twin doors that have no glass windows.

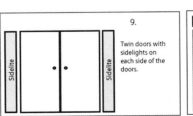
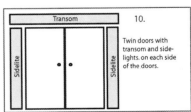

Door Styles

Door styles are an important ingredient in the entryway, but it doesn't end there. Adding other architectural features further enhances the entryway. Healthy and trimmed plants in decorative containers and in the landscaped area around the entryway add to the finished look. An enhanced walkway and/or steps leading up to the entryway go a long way toward enhancing the area. So, as we review the different types of doors, these features will be discussed. The pictures of the doors are in the order and locations shown in the table at the left.

1. The basic single door with no window and no accents is the type of door most often seen. It is usually paneled, and can be made from a variety of grades of wood, vinyl, fiberglass or metal. It is weatherproof, painted or stained, provides privacy and security, and meets all the basic needs for a door.

Charleston, South Carolina

The 12-panel arched door and magnificent surround combination with a small balcony. On either side of the door are coach lights, urns with floral arrangements, and arched windows. The handrails along the landing area are trimmed with manicured bushes. Red flowers, a curved walkway, and manicured grass complete the entryway.
Shorewood (Milwaukee), Wisconsin

Ashville, North Carolina

This four-panel door has panels that have raised trim. The door has a decorative surround and there is a brick walkway and steps leading up to it. The door has been enhanced with a cascading floral arrangement and a black doorknocker. Two urns with ferns embellish the walkway.
Winchester, Kentucky

The six-panel door is a tan color matching the shutters on the windows and other trim on the house. The door has a decorative wreath with cascading flowers and is framed with an elegant surround. Two urns with brightly colored flowers and two coach lights balance each side of the entryway. The ivy has been trimmed and allowed to grow across the front of the lower step.
Winchester, Kentucky

7

The unique paneled door is artistically framed with a surround, and has small windows framed with surrounds on each side. The door is embellished with a wreath, and pots with topiary on each side. Stairs that lead up to the landing are bordered by welcoming pineapple sculptures.
Shorewood (Milwaukee), Wisconsin

This one-of-a-kind recessed eight-paneled carved door is V-shaped. Treated wood creates an elaborate frame around the door.
House on the Rock, Wisconsin

The Oriental door is finished in white, has been decorated with an elaborate design, and has a bubble glass that contains an artistic sculpture.
House on the Rock, Wisconsin

The six-panel door is unique, without a noticeable frame around the door. It has been decorated with a floral wreath and matching urns with floral arrangements. There are steps and a landing built with rock. Notice the welcoming pineapple sculpture.
Wisconsin Dells, Wisconsin

2. This is a single door with no window but with a transom above. The transom can be made with glass or can be solid, stationary or operational. Transoms have three distinct shapes: arch, ellipse, and box.

The eight-paneled door has contrasting colors and has a frame with the same contrasting colors. There is a decorated, arched, fan-shaped transom above. Blooming plants line the walkway.
Savannah, Georgia

The twelve-paneled door has an arched transom. The elaborate surround around the door includes matching columns and the topper has an arabesque design.
Ashville, North Carolina

The four-paneled door has a transom with the address displayed in gold colored numbers. Over the doorway is a roof with corbels. Matching coach light fixtures are on each side of the door. Stair railings match the door framing.
Folly Beach, South Carolina

The six-panel door with glass transom is a lighter color gray that matches the house, doorframe, and brickwork on the steps and house. A group of planters with small plants are set off to the right with a coach lamp above.
Clinton, Tennessee

The six-panel red door has a gold colored kick plate, a gold colored doorknocker, and an art glass transom above the door. This is all framed with a white surround.
Frankfort, Kentucky

The six-panel door with a transom, the railings, and the shutters are all the same off-white color giving the entryway a clean look. Coach lights on both sides of the doorway finish the decor.
Frankfort, Kentucky

Steps lead up to the door with a transom. The door is the same color as the decoration below the roofline on the front of the porch.
Oak Park, Illinois

The five-panel door and arched transom are enclosed with an arched surround. A magnificent urn containing flowers is displayed in the landscape in front of the landing. A railing and landscaping enclose the entryway.
Rockford, Illinois

An old brick walkway and low stoop lead up to the six-panel front door. The elegant surround around the door has a four-panel cut glass transom. This is finished off with a coach lamp to the left of the door.
Shorewood (Milwaukee), Wisconsin

3. This door has no transom but has a single sidelight. The sidelight may be on either side of the door. The sidelight is usually stationary but can be operational and can include screening.

A single step leads up to the six-panel door and sidelight with etched glass.
Danville, Illinois

This eight-paneled door has a sidelight with three panes of glass.
Beloit, Wisconsin

The six-panel door has a sidelight with several panes of glass. The chair with birdhouses is a fun addition to the entryway.
Rockford, Illinois

11

4. This style of single door has no transom but has a sidelight on each side of the door. The sidelights are usually stationary but can be operational and include screening.

The six-panel door is red in contrast to the white sidelights and surround. The acorn pediment on the surround, the brick steps, railings, and potted flowers add charm and grace to the entryway.
Charleston, South Carolina

Driving past this home, this is the only front door visible.
Ashville, North Carolina

Zooming in on the door you can see that it is special. It appears to be a carved door and has sidelights. It is under a grand stone arch with a matching stone walkway leading up to it. Railings have been added separating the landscaping from the entryway
Ashville, North Carolina

The six-panel door has sidelights that are trimmed in a gold color matching the hardware on the door.
Clinton, Tennessee

This intimate columned entryway has a welcoming appearance further enhanced by the two comfortable chairs and four potted plants.
Winchester, Kentucky

This entryway is bordered by shuttered windows and manicured hedges.
Georgetown, Kentucky

This paneled door with sidelights has a surround with an acorn pediment. The coach light, floral wreath, urn with flowers, and blooming plants complement the entryway.
Georgetown, Kentucky

Coming in closer we can see the arched entryway contains a paneled door with sidelights.
Georgetown, Kentucky

The white surround sets off the six-paneled door with paneled sidelights. This setting is further decorated with a brick step, flowers, white urns, and two glowing coach lights.
Georgetown, Kentucky

Tucked back inside the arched brick entryway is a panel door with sidelights. The wreath on the door and plants growing around the area complement the chair holding an overflowing fern.
Danville, Illinois

13

The dark colored door with full length glass sidelights is made even cozier by the variety of flowering plants framing the steps approaching the entryway.
Danville, Illinois

The entryway has a surround with a parapet on top. The six-panel door with curtained sidelights, the handrails, brick step, two coach light fixtures, ceiling light, and potted flowering plant complete the picture. The opened working shutters on the windows above complement the whole scene.
Rockford, Illinois

The six-panel white door has two sidelights that are green and has an open pediment. The two numbers over the door and two mailboxes suggest two residences inside.
Wisconsin Dells, Wisconsin

5. Another option would be a single door with a transom above and a single sidelight on either side of the door. There is no sample picture of this style of door in this book.

14

6. The last examples for a single door have a transom above and sidelights on both sides of the door.

An attractive entryway is created with this four-panel door with transom and two sidelights. A great contribution is the roof with corbels that doubles as a small porch above. The corbels, hanging lamp, potted plants, and old brick paving all add up to an extremely appealing entryway.
Savannah, Georgia

The single black door with an arched transom and sidelights is inset in a pediment gabled surround. The used brick walkway and steps are topped with curved metal handrails. Coach lamps are on both sides of the framing.
Charleston, South Carolina

At the top of the stairs stands a six-panel door with arched transom and full-length glass sidelights. The scene has two coach lights and a recessed overhead light.
Charleston, South Carolina

A six-panel door has an arched fan transom and two sidelights. Matching poles hold up a pedimented roof.
Flat Rock, North Carolina

The reflecting sun illuminates the red six-panel door with an arched fan transom and two sidelights. The entryway is shaded with a small roof with four support columns. The landing is brick and the walkway is stone.
Ashville, North Carolina

15

The six-panel door has a transom and two full-length glass sidelights. Urns with topiary complete the picture
Clinton, Tennessee

The six-panel door has arch transom and full length glass sidelights. The effect if further complemented by the arch in the roof over the entryway and the four post supports.
Clinton, Tennessee

16

The six-panel door has a transom and full-length glass sidelights. An extended living area is created with the use of wicker chairs and potted flowering plants.
Clinton, Tennessee

This six-panel door with transom and sidelights has a surround
Frankfort, Kentucky

This door has a solid transom and two glass sidelights. They are nicely framed with a roof with a broken pediment filled with an arch. The unique feature is the double support poles. The hanging coach lamp further complements the poles, along with double handrails on the steps and the curved walkway.
Frankfort, Kentucky

17

A graceful entryway is created around the six-panel door with arched transom and sidelights. Hanging plants add color and the curved metal handrail offers assistance up the stairs.
Frankfort, Kentucky

The six-panel door with arched transom and sidelights is complemented by the use of a wreath, flowering potted plants, and black metal handrail.
Georgetown, Kentucky

This arched entryway shades the six-panel door with transom and sidelights.
Georgetown, Kentucky

The introduction to the entryway is a stunning circular porch.
Georgetown, Kentucky

The six-panel door has an arched transom and side panels.
Georgetown, Kentucky

The porch roof of the entryway creates a base for the upstairs porch.
Turkey Run State Park, Indiana

The eight-panel door has a transom and sidelights.
Turkey Run State Park, Indiana

The eight-panel door is framed by the transom and matching sidelights. The edges of the stairs are nicely hidden by the plants in the landscaping and the potted flowering plants.
Bloomington, Illinois

19

The broken pediment roofline allows us to see the eight-panel door with solid transom and special sidelights.
Beloit, Wisconsin

The six-panel door is recessed behind the arched entry that has lit coach lamps and urns with flowers on either side. A ceiling lamp illuminates the six-panel door with cut glass transom and sidelights.
Rockford, Illinois

The eight-panel door has a multi-paneled transom and sidelights that match the windows above.
Rockford, Illinois

The six-panel door has a multi-paneled transom and sidelights. Urns with blooming plants decorate the entryway.
Rockford, Illinois

This four-panel door with transom and sidelights is tucked neatly back in an alcove lined with matching panels.
Wisconsin Dells, Wisconsin

7. Section 7 is the beginning of the pictures of twin doors. The first doors are twin doors with no glass in the doors and there are no accents (transom or sidelight) around them.

These arched twin doors adorn a dramatic entryway. Notice the matching posts on either side of the doors and the gate to the driveway.
Charleston, South Carolina

Twin six-panel doors complement an entryway given special treatment with tiled steps and walkway, roof capped columns, and an arched dormer above.
Rockford, Illinois

Twin doors are tucked back in the shade with each door containing sixteen panels. The doors are painted in a way to highlight the panel feature.
Winchester, Kentucky

21

Twin doors are set back under a balcony trimmed with flower boxes.
Rockford, Illinois

Twin six-panel doors are tucked back into a surround with a parapet and bordered by matching columns. Brick steps lead up to the doors.
Rockford, Illinois

Twin doors have been decorated with sculptures, potted plants, and standing light fixtures. Coach lamps are ready to provide more lighting on either side of the doors.
Beloit, Wisconsin

8. Twin doors have a transom made with glass or solid above them.

The arched opening over the entryway frames the artfully paneled double doors with arched transom. The hanging lamp and ferns complete the decor.
Mission, Texas

Go through the gate and up the brick steps to the porch entryway with twin two-panel doors and a transom.
Savannah, Georgia

The elegant twin doors on the second level have a transom with a door topper above.
Savannah, Georgia

Typical of many homes in Savannah, there are two levels for entry, one above the other.
Savannah, Georgia

The ornate carved twin doors with transom on this second level are in a covered entryway with lacy handrails.
Savannah, Georgia

As I was walking down the street approaching this house I knew it would be something special.
Charleston, South Carolina

The twin doors with arched transom are a work of art. The surround around the doors is luxurious. The stylish urns contain topiary. Down the steps are potted plants to complete the landscaped entryway.
Charleston, Couth Carolina

At the curb is a hitching post preserved from days gone by.
Charleston, Couth Carolina

An elegant circular porch graces the entryway.
Evanston, Indiana

The twin doors have circular panels with raised trim and a roof with corbels. The flat roof overhead also serves as a small balcony.
Evanston, Indiana

Twin doors have a transom and a door topper above.
Rockford, Illinois

The entryway has twin five-panel doors with transom and a gold colored doorknocker on each door. A coach lamp hangs from above.
Oak Park, Illinois

25

The bright sunlight lights up the flowers that line the walkway.
Rockford, Illinois

Twin doors with a transom are framed with shutters. Twin windows are on each side of the doorway. Chairs offer a resting place. The pillars in front have graceful urns with cascading flowers.
Rockford, Illinois

9. Twin doors have a sidelight on each side of the doors.

The twin doors have two sidelights under a magnificent entryway.
Savannah, Georgia

The twin doors are framed with sidelights and a transom with plate glass.
Rockford, Illinois

The twin doors have two sidelights with sparkling bevel windows.
Beloit, Wisconsin

10. Twin doors have a transom above them made with glass or solid and a sidelight on each side of the doors.

Doors with Windows and Accents

Exterior Door Sketches

Doors with Windows and Accents

The simple sketches of doors below show the basic variety of configurations for doors with windows. The doors themselves can be plain, paneled, or carved and decorated. The windows can be made in a variety of sizes and shapes. Transoms basicly have three distinct shapes: arch, ellipse and box. Sidelights can be made in a variety of shapes and sizes. Door hardware is available in a large variety of materials, colors, shapes and sizes.

Single doors that have glass windows.

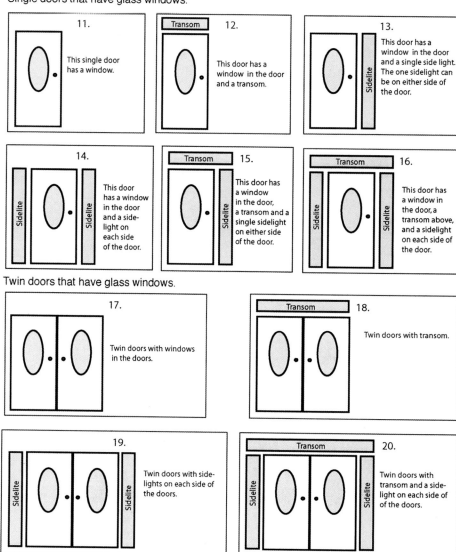

11.
This single door has a window.

12.
Transom
This door has a window in the door and a transom.

13.
This door has a window in the door and a single side light. The one sidelight can be on either side of the door.
Sidelite

14.
Sidelite
This door has a window in the door and a side-light on each side of the door.
Sidelite

15.
Transom
This door has a window in the door, a transom and a single sidelight on either side of the door.
Sidelite

16.
Transom
This door has a window in the door, a transom above, and a sidelight on each side of the door.
Sidelite
Sidelite

Twin doors that have glass windows.

17.
Twin doors with windows in the doors.

18.
Transom
Twin doors with transom.

19.
Sidelite
Twin doors with side-lights on each side of the doors.
Sidelite

20.
Transom
Sidelite
Twin doors with transom and a side-light on each side of of the doors.
Sidelite

28

Doors with Windows and Accents

11. The eleventh door type is the beginning of the pictures of doors with windows. Some doors have more than one window. The first examples have a window(s), but no accents (transom or sidelight).

Circular stepping-stones lead up to the front entryway of this Spanish style home.
Brownsville, Texas

This single door has two arched windows. The door and matching frame appear to be metal.
Pearsall, Texas

The single front door is arched and is inset and framed with a tiled archway.
Brownsville, Texas

This single door has a circular window and is inset and framed with inset tiles.
Brownsville, Texas

The single door has an oval window and is decorated on each side with shutters and lamps.
Beaufort, South Carolina

The single door has an oval window with art glass. The entryway is decorated with a large frog statue and a potted flowering plant. A strawberry pot is resting on one of the brick steps.
Folly Beach, South Carolina

The single door has an oval window accented in white.
Beaufort, South Carolina

The single door has a large geometric glass window, a gold colored kick plate, and is framed by louvered shutters.
Folly Beach, South Carolina

The single door has two panels and a geometric glass window.
Oak Ridge, Tennessee

31

The single, four-panel door has an arched window at the top.
Winchester, Kentucky

The single door has an oval art glass window decorated with a wreath.
Georgetown, Kentucky

The single door has a geometric window.
Georgetown, Kentucky

The single door has an oval etched glass window.
Georgetown, Kentucky

The single door has raised trim and a glass window decorated with a wreath. The door is framed by an elegant surround.
Georgetown, Kentucky

The slab porch and step are covered with ceramic tile. The cozy seating area has white wicker furniture and planter, and a hanging pot of flowers.
Georgetown, Kentucky

The single six-panel door has a square window centered in the door.
Georgetown, Kentucky

The entryway is decorated with black wicker furniture that matches the wrought iron balconies above. An exquisite urn with a topiary stands at the front of the porch.
Evansville, Indiana

Single arched door has an art glass window and a surround.
Evansville, Indiana

The single door has an art glass oval window.
Princeton, Indiana

The magnificent entryway is set with a slab porch with a low balustrade, sweeping steps, and a large bush guarding each side.
Bloomington, Illinois

The single door has an art glass oval window.
Danville, Illinois

The single door has three equal sized windows with a row of five dowels in each. A lit coach lamp is overhead and substantial urns with blooming plants adorn the entryway.
Bloomington, Illinois

The single wood door with six paned glass windows is framed with a contrasting stone frame, covered with a flat copper roof that appears to be floating. Stone planter areas and steps lead up to an entryway patio. Square pots with plants sit on each side of the door. Shutters that match the door are on the windows.
Bloomington, Illinois

The single arched door has an arched paned glass window. A gabled roof has supporting corbels. Guardrails topped with urns with flowering plants sit on both sides of the door.
Shorewood (Milwaukee), Wisconsin

Tucked back in a small alcove is a single door with a small triangular window. The door is beautifully decorated with a simple geometric pattern.
Shorewood (Milwaukee), Wisconsin

The single arched door with two small windows is inset in an arched marble surround. The framing is a rich contrast to the brick wall.
Shorewood (Milwaukee), Wisconsin

This single door has four stacked windows with frosted drapery glass. The door is framed with inset and sculptured stones having a variety of subjects.
Franklin (Milwaukee), Wisconsin

This single eleven-panel door has a small art glass window in the twelfth panel.
Franklin (Milwaukee), Wisconsin

35

This single seventeen-panel door has a small art glass window in the eighteenth panel.
Dallas, Oregon

This single seven-panel door has an arched window with a geometric design in the center panel.
San Diego, California

This single door has irises in the art glass window.
San Diego, California

12. The single door has a window(s) and a transom above it.

This entryway has an arched window theme.
Hildago, Texas

Georgetown, Kentucky

The single door has a glass window and a transom above, all contained in a matching surround. The frame and door are ornately carved. A coach lamp hangs from above.
Georgetown, Kentucky

The single door has an art glass window and transom above. The door is ornately carved. A lit coach lamp hangs from above.
Evansville, Indiana

The single four-panel door has an arched window with paned glass and a solid transom above. Above the doorway is an arched door topper.
Shorewood (Milwaukee), Wisconsin

A paved walkway meanders up to the entryway.
Franklin (Milwaukee), Wisconsin

The single door with glass is topped with a solid peaked transom and they are all framed in a matching peaked surround. The steps match the walkway.
Franklin (Milwaukee), Wisconsin

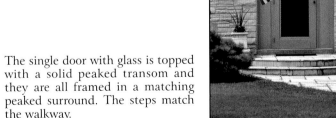

13. The single door has a window(s) and a single sidelight. The one sidelight may be on either side of the door.

The single three-panel door has a window with glass at the top. To the right is a sidelight with full length matching glass.
Dallas, Oregon

The single door with art glass window has a sidelight on the left. The panels in the alcove match the door. Note that the door and frame are taller than the sidelight and panels.
Charleston, South Carolina

The single door has matching windows with etched glass and a matching sidelight.
Trempealeau, Wisconsin

14. The single door has a window(s) and sidelights on both sides of the door.

The single door has an arched window and arched sidelights.
Laredo, Texas

The single door with an arched cut glass window has sidelights with cut glass windows.
Brownsville, Texas

The single door with an arched cut glass window has sidelights all framed in dark framing.
Hendersonville, North Carolina

The single door with sparkling cut glass oval window and matching sidelights are in an entryway that also has an oval paned glass window. The slab porch and steps are bordered with brickwork that matches the house.
Clinton, Tennessee

The single door with an art glass window has matching sidelights.
Clinton, Tennessee

The single door has an art glass window and contrasting colored sidelights with matching windows.
Clinton, Tennessee

The single door has a cut glass window and matching sidelights.
Clinton, Tennessee

The single door has a large oval sparkling cut glass window with sidelights with cut glass windows.
Georgetown, Kentucky

The entryway is spruced up with four urns containing flowering plants. The shiny floor reflects the doorway and welcoming side chairs.
Georgetown, Kentucky

The single door has a cut glass window with sidelights. The entryway has an awning providing the shade.
Georgetown, Kentucky

The single door has a large window decorated with a cascade of flowers. The sidelights have panes of glass—the top panes are special. The doorway has coach lamps on both sides.
Georgetown, Kentucky

The door has an oval with art glass and the sidelights match.
Danville, Illinois

The door has two windows with art glass and the sidelights match.
Danville, Illinois

The door has a window with art glass and the sidelights match.
Rockford, Illinois

This single door has large sidelights that appear to have screens suggesting that the sidelights can be opened to bring in fresh air.
Rockford, Illinois

The door has a window with cut glass and the sidelights match.
Rockford, Illinois

The single door with a full-length art glass window has two sidelights. The entryway is made up with a gabled roofed pediment with supporting columns.
Wisconsin Dells, Wisconsin

A curved walkway leads up to a slab porch with natural wood railings and walls. The single door has an oval window and sidelights with full-length windows. Pots and urns with flowers and plants decorate the entryway.
Dallas, Oregon

The single door has a large art glass oval window and arched sidelights.
Dallas, Oregon

15. The single door has a window(s), a transom above, and a single sidelight on either side of the door.

The single door has a large window with art glass, a transom above with matching art glass, and a single sidelight with art glass that also matches.
Dallas, Oregon

The single door has a window with art glass and sidelights with art glass.
Independence, Oregon

The single door has a window with art glass, a glass transom above, and a single sidelight with art glass. The window in the door has a decorative wreath. Pots of flowering plants add color to the entryway.
Georgetown, Kentucky

Dallas, Oregon

16. The single door has a window(s), a transom above, and a sidelight on each side of the door.

The meandering walkway leads up to the entryway of this newly built house. Notice the windows to the left of the entryway.
Hildago, Texas

The single door has two panels, five small windows and one long window down the middle of the door. There are two full-length glass sidelights and there is a large arched transom above the door and sidelights. This is all enclosed in an arched alcove entryway.
Hildago, Texas

A single door with a full-length glass window has a white frame with sidelights and a triple-window transom.
Charleston, South Carolina

The single door has raised borders on the panels, and a window that matches the sidelight windows. Above the door and sidelights is a glass transom.
Clinton, Tennessee

At the top of the steps is an entryway containing a door with a large oval etched window, glass transom, and wide etched glass sidelights.
Folly Beach, South Carolina

43

The tall arched entryway, solid brick design on the wall, and arched windows create and interesting affect. A whole section is devoted to high entryways later in the book.
Clinton, Tennessee

Inside the entryway is a single panel door with an arched narrow window. The door has sidelights and there is a large multi-pane glass transom above.
Clinton, Tennessee

The gable roof contains an arch over the entryway and is supported by two sets of columns.
Clinton, Tennessee

The single door with white trim contains a large oval window with art glass. Above is a large transom with matching art glass and to the sides of the door are full-length sidelights with more matching art glass. Bricks create an arch surround around the door.
Clinton, Tennessee

A single door with two windows containing art glass has matching sidelights. Above them is an arched transom.
Clinton, Tennessee

A view of the front of the house shows, among other things, a window with sidelights on the second floor above the entryway.
Oak Ridge, Tennessee

Under an open gable roof is a single door with a large oval glass window and frameless multi-paned sidelights and large transom above.
Clinton, Tennessee

The hip roofed stoop shades a single door with art glass and sidelights that match the sidelights in the window above. Above the door is a multi-paned transom.

A single door with a large art glass window has multi-paned sidelights and transom.
Oak Ridge, Tennessee

Here we have a single door with an oval window, sidelights, and transom.

This single door with glass window has a transom and sidelights. The entire white frame has unique accents. Above is a roof with corbels. The top of the roof has ornamental metal guardrails.
Georgetown, Kentucky

Tucked back into an arched alcove entryway is a single dark door with art glass that matches those in the two sidelights. Above them is a transom with art glass. These are framed with a brick arched surround.
Georgetown, Kentucky

The large single door with a glass window has an arched cut glass transom and sidelights. Above the doorframe is a door topper that matches the arch over the entryway. Notice the detail on the capital at the top of the column. An elegant planted urn is at the base of the column.
Bloomington, Illinois

The single door has two windows, two sidelights with matching sized windows, and a transom. They have matching beveled art glass.
Orfordville, Wisconsin

The high-reaching entryway is filled with the single door with full-length cut glass window and sidelights. The glass transom above fills the top of the entryway.
Janesville, Wisconsin

The single door has a full-length glass window, large sidelights, and an arched transom made up with three parts. Another thing that is interesting is the different colors in the entryway, including the roof of the entryway, and the treatment around the windows.
Shorewood (Milwaukee), Wisconsin

The single door has a full-length glass window with a geometric pattern on it. The sidelights have glass of equal length to the door. Above the door and sidelights is a glass transom and above that is a glass-block window.
Wisconsin Dells, Wisconsin

17. Twin doors with glass and no accents around them.

The twin doors are French doors with beveled glass and wood mullions. Ferns hang on both sides of the doors.
Lexington, Kentucky

A used brick walkway takes us up to the large stoop and twin doors with glass windows. Two urns with blooming plants are placed on each side of the walkway near the stoop.
Lexington, Kentucky

Tall twin doors with panels and glass windows sit back in the alcove frame covered with a flat-roof. Pots with flowering plants rest on sculptured cherub plant stands at the bottom of the entryway steps.
Georgetown, Kentucky

These twin doors have glass windows.
Frankfort, Kentucky

A close-up of one of the urns reveals the detail in the urn and pedestal.
Lexington, Kentucky

48

The curved driveway sweeps past the fountain and the full-length front porch to the front entryway and door of this palatial home.
Bloomington, Illinois

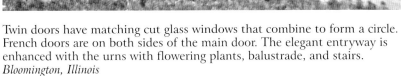

Twin doors have cut glass and etched windows.
Orfordville, Wisconsin

Twin doors have matching cut glass windows that combine to form a circle. French doors are on both sides of the main door. The elegant entryway is enhanced with the urns with flowering plants, balustrade, and stairs.
Bloomington, Illinois

An engaging entryway has been created around the simple twin doors with glass windows.
Dallas, Oregon

18. Twin doors with a window(s) and a transom above them.

At the top of the stairway are twin metal doors with sculptured art. A very large paned window above resembles a transom. The doors and transom are all contained in the brick frame created by the diagonal lines of brick.
Laredo, Texas

Twin doors have arched glass windows and a paneled transom above. An urn with a blooming plant rests on the landing.
Savannah, Georgia

This alcove entryway has twin French doors with plate glass and twin transom windows.
Rockford, Illinois

The twin doors have art glass windows and an arched transom.
Danville, Illinois

These twin doors have arched windows and an arched transom above. The entryway is shaded with a flat roof that is supported by pillars and topped with an ornamental parapet.
Savannah, Georgia

This entryway welcomes us with twin doors and flowers, but the obvious resting place is on the balcony above. There to enjoy is antique wrought iron railings, pots of flowers, and comfortable seating.
Bloomington, Illinois

The twin doors have windows with geometric framed panes and an arched transom.
Bloomington, Illinois

Twin doors with art glass have a transom above.
Wisconsin Dells, Wisconsin

The entryway is shaded with a high gabled roof supported with pillars.
Dallas, Oregon

Twin doors with plate glass and transom made up with three windows.
Dallas, Oregon

19. Twin doors with windows and sidelights.

This breathtaking entryway is decorated with flowering plants in urns, gentle steps, and a balcony above that is sheltered by a curved roof.
Rockford, Illinois

The arch above the doorway and the steps leading up to the door create an appealing visual affect.
Rockford, Illinois

Twin doors with art glass windows and two sidelights on each side of the doors create an impressive appearance.
Rockford, Illinois

20. Twin doors with windows, a transom above, and sidelights.

Twin French doors with full-length plate glass have tall sidelights and a transom over only the doors. The brick steps and handrails add to the appeal of the entryway.
Hilton Head, South Carolina

Hilton Head, South Carolina

Twin doors with beveled glass windows, sidelights, and arched transom are framed with a continuous frame that is arched. The bench, slate walkway and porch, brick trimmed steps, and stately porch columns are topped with a balcony.
Charleston, South Carolina

Approaching this home the first thing I noticed was the brick walkways and the pediment roof and four distinctive ionic columns.
Georgetown, Kentucky

Looking past the ionic columns the twin doors with glass plate windows, sidelights, and arched transom can be seen.
Georgetown, Kentucky

Twin doors with bevel glass windows are inset in a frame of sidelights with plate glass and a transom with art glass.
Bloomington, Illinois

Twin French doors with full length plate glass have matching sidelights. Above is a large transom, and they are all framed in a continuous brick frame.
Rockford, Illinois

Chapter II. Outer Doors

In Section I, the doors were shown without any outer doors such as security doors, storm doors, screen doors, or louvered doors. If the main door to the house doesn't have an outer door in front of it, it looks really great, but doesn't have the flexibility that outer doors provide. Modern outer doors can be attractive and add to the overall entryway appearance while providing the flexibility to leave the inner door open. They provide security, and at the same time allow light and fresh air to enter the house. Searching the Internet for these types of doors will provide all kinds of information about today's product designs.

The pictures that follow show you a few examples I found while searching out interesting entryways. While you are looking at the outer doors, remember what you've learned about entryways and doors, transoms, and sidelights in the previous sections.

1. Security Doors:

Security doors can look a lot like metal gates. They usually have dead-bolt locks. They are installed outside the prime, or inside, door. A locked security door provides a double protection for an entryway when the occupants opens the inside door or when leaving the inside door standing open. Some security doors have their own metal mesh screening. These doors allow airflow when the inside door is in the open position and can be an alternative to screen doors.

Security doors are important for peace of mind when it comes to an outer door. They are made with their own sturdy frame and are not too difficult to install. One of the websites that offers a lot of information is http://www.home-security-doors.info/. Check out the "FAQ's" under "Security Doors."

Security Door
Savannah, Georgia

This classy gate and fence are also performing the function of a security door.
Charleston, South Carolina

Security Door
Savannah, Georgia

Security door
Georgetown, Kentucky

Security door
Evansville, Indiana

Twin security doors
Evansville, Indiana

Arched security/storm door
Bloomington, Illinois

Arched security door
Oak Park, Illinois

Security door
Lake Geneva, Wisconsin

Security door
Rockford, Illinois

Security door
Rockford, Illinois

Security door
Rockford, Illinois

57

Security door
Rockford, Illinois

Security door
Rockford, Illinois

Twin security doors
Rockford, Illinois

2. Storm Doors:

A storm door fits over and protects your prime door and provides important insulation in the winter and summer. A storm door and your prime door act in tandem to create a dead air space between the doors. This reduces heat loss in the winter and heat gain in summer, lowering energy costs. The first series of pictures that follow are the popular single glass pane storm doors.

Single glass pane storm door
Clinton, Tennessee

Single glass pane storm door
Charleston, South Carolina

Single glass pane storm door
Winchester, Kentucky

Single glass pane storm door
Charleston, South Carolina

Twin single glass pane storm doors
Winchester, Kentucky

59

Single glass pane storm door
Winchester, Kentucky

Single glass pane storm door
Versailes, Kentucky

Single glass pane storm door
Versailes, Kentucky

Single glass pane storm door
Versailes, Kentucky

Single glass pane storm door
Georgetown, Kentucky

Single glass pane storm door
Georgetown, Kentucky

Single glass pane storm door
Georgetown, Kentucky

Single glass pane storm door
Georgetown, Kentucky

Single glass pane storm door
Danville, Illinois

Single glass pane storm door
Evansville, Indiana

Single glass pane storm door.
Bloomington, Illinois

Single glass pane storm door
Danville, Illinois

Single glass pane storm door
Orfordville, Wisconsin

Single glass pane storm door
Orfordville, Wisconsin

Single glass pane storm door
Beloit, Wisconsin

Single glass pane storm door
Beloit, Wisconsin

Single glass pane storm door
South Beloit, Illinois

Single glass pane storm door
Shorewood (Milwaukee), Wisconsin

63

Single glass pane storm door
Shorewood (Milwaukee), Wisconsin

Single glass pane wood storm door
Shorewood (Milwaukee), Wisconsin

Single glass pane storm door
Lake Geneva, Wisconsin

Single glass pane storm door
Rockford, Illinois

Single glass pane storm door
Rockford, Illinois

Single glass pane storm door
Rockford, Illinois

Twin glass pane storm doors
Rockford, Illinois

Single glass pane storm door
Rockford, Illinois

Single glass pane storm door
Beloit, Wisconsin

Twin glass pane storm doors
Wisconsin Dells, Wisconsin

Twin glass pane storm doors
Rockford, Illinois

Single glass pane storm door
Independence, Oregon

Other styles of storm doors have a single or double pane of glass, one above the other. Often one or both panes are removable and can be replaced with a screen panel. Storm glass doors provide a second layer to the front door to help hold out the cold and wet weather. They have a lock and provide a level of security when the inside door is open. The next series of pictures show a variety of storm doors other than the single glass pane storm doors.

Storm door
Georgetown, Kentucky

Storm door
Winchester, Kentucky

Storm door
Georgetown, Kentucky

Arched storm
Frankfort, Kentucky

Storm door
Georgetown, Kentucky

67

Storm door
Shorewood (Milwaukee), Wisconsin

Arched storm door
Evansville, Indiana

Storm door
Sullivan, Indiana

Arched storm door
Shorewood (Milwaukee), Wisconsin

Storm door
Shorewood (Milwaukee), Wisconsin

Storm door
Shorewood (Milwaukee), Wisconsin

Storm door
*Shorewood (Milwaukee),
Wisconsin*

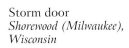

Storm door
Rockford, Illinois

Storm door
Rockford, Illinois

Storm door
Rockford, Illinois

Storm door
Wisconsin Dells, Wisconsin

Storm door
Wisconsin Dells,
Wisconsin

Storm door
Wisconsin Dells, Wisconsin

3. Screen Doors:

Screen doors have a lock that provides a level of security. The screen eliminates most insects, and allows light and airflow when the prime door is open.

Screen door
Bloomington, Illinois

Screen door
Evansville, Indiana

Screen door
Bloomington, Illinois

Screen door
Princeton, Indiana

Arched screen door
Bloomington, Illinois

Screen door
Bloomington, Illinois

Arched screen door
Shorewood (Milwaukee), Wisconsin

Screen door
Orfordville, Wisconsin

Screen door
Beloit, Wisconsin

Screen door
Shorewood (Milwaukee), Wisconsin

Screen door
Rockford, Illinois

Screen door
Shorewood (Milwaukee), Wisconsin

Screen door
Rockford, Illinois

A closer view of the solid shell shaped transom.
Shorewood (Milwaukee), Wisconsin

Screen door
Rockford, Illinois

73

Screen door
Wisconsin Dells, Wisconsin

Arched screen door
Dallas, Oregon

Screen door
Wisconsin Dells, Wisconsin

Arched screen door
Dallas, Oregon

4. Louver Doors:

Louver doors or shutters installed over the prime door are an attractive option. The louver doors provide privacy, security when locked, and allow airflow. Under the right circumstances, twin louver doors can be installed so they can swing open 180 degrees. When installed that way they can be secured against the wall on either side of the doorway providing a decorative appearance to the entryway. More installations of this type are shown in my book *1000 Shutters and Awnings*.

Louvered shutter door
Ashville, North Carolina

Louvered shutter door
Ashville, North Carolina

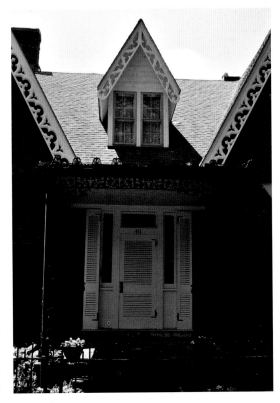

Louvered shutter door
Frankfort, Kentucky

Louvered shutter door
Georgetown, Kentucky

Louvered shutter door
Rockford, Illinois

Back in the shade is an entryway with shutters in the open position.
Bloomington, Illinois

Louvered shutter door
Rockford, Illinois

Chapter III. Types of Entryways

Types of Entryways

This section is about the *layout or design* of the entryway and the areas leading up to it. Presented here are layouts of increasing complexity, beginning with the simplest designs and progressing to the ever more complex. When viewing each picture, notice the arrangement of the entryway, the style of door, the area around it, and the way the whole area has been decorated and improved. The entryways will appear as shown in the chart above.

1.(a.) **Door Entryway:**

The doors that are shown here are flush with the wall of the house and have little or no roof over them.

Door entryway
Flat Rock, North Carolina

Door entryway
Rockford, Illinois

Door entryway
Winchester, Kentucky

Door entryway
Rockford, Illinois

Door entryway
Wisconsin Dells, Wisconsin

Door entryway
Oak Park (Chicago), Illinois

Door entryway
Dallas, Oregon

Door entryway
Dallas, Oregon

Door entryway
Dallas, Oregon

Door entryway
Dallas, Oregon

Door entryway
Dallas, Oregon

1.(b.) Door Entryway with Stone Trim:

The doors that are shown here are similar to those shown in 1.(a.) except they have been enhanced with inlaid stone trim around the door.

Door entryway with stone trim
Bloomington, Illinois

Door entryway with stone trim
Oak Park (Chicago), Illinois

Door entryway with stone trim
Oak Park (Chicago), Illinois

Door entryway with stone trim
Oak Park (Chicago), Illinois

80

Door entryway with stone trim
Shorewood (Milwaukee), Wisconsin

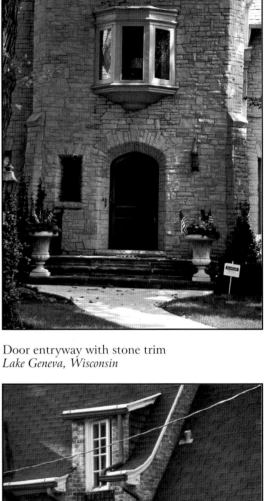

Door entryway with stone trim
Lake Geneva, Wisconsin

Door
entryway
with
stone
trim
*Lake
Geneva,
Wisconsin*

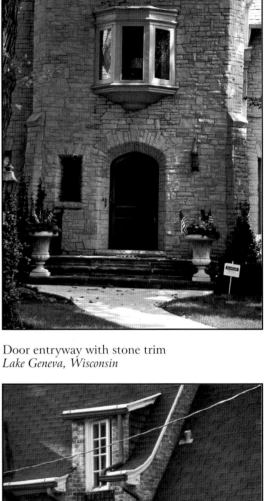

Door entryway with stone trim
Beloit, Wisconsin

1.(c.) Door Entryway Surrounds:

The doors shown here are flush or nearly flush with the wall of the house and have a decorative surround around the door.

Door entryway with surround
Mackinac Island, Michigan

Door entryway with surround
Charleston, South Carolina

Door entryway with surround
Ashville, North Carolina

Door entryway with surround
Winchester, Kentucky

Door entryway with surround
Frankfort, Kentucky

Door entryway with surround
Winchester, Kentucky

Door entryway with surround
Evansville, Indiana

Door entryway with surround
Lexington, Kentucky

Door entryway with surround
Bloomington, Illinois

Door entryway with surround
Oak Park (Chicago), Illinois

Door entryway with surround
Bloomington, Illinois

Door entryway with surround
Oak Park (Chicago), Illinois

Door entryway with surround
Shorewood (Milwaukee), Wisconsin

Door entryway with surround
Oak Park (Chicago), Illinois

Door entryway with surround
Franklin (Milwaukee), Wisconsin

Door entryway with surround
Beloit, Wisconsin

Door entryway with surround
Rockford, Illinois

Door entryway with surround
Dallas, Oregon

1.(d.) Door Entryway with Small Roof (stoop):

The doors shown here are similar to the doors in 1.(a.) except that they have a roof above the door that provides some shelter from the weather and adds dimension to the entryway. Some have steps and a landing.

Door entryway with small roof
Savannah, Georgia

Door entryway with small roof
Beaufort, South Carolina

Door entryway with surround
Dallas, Oregon

Door entryway with small roof
Savannah, Georgia

Door entryway with small roof
Beaufort, South Carolina

Door entryway with small roof
Frankfort, Kentucky

Door entryway with small roof
Bloomington, Illinois

Door entryway with small roof
Beloit, Wisconsin

Door entryway with small roof
Evansville, Indiana

1.(e.) Door Entryway Recessed:

The doorways in these pictures have been recessed back through the wall of the house, creating an alcove.

Door entryway recessed
Evansville, Indiana

Door entryway recessed
Evansville, Indiana

Door entryway recessed.
Ashville, North Carolina

Door entryway recessed
Bloomington, Illinois

Door entryway recessed
Rockford, Illinois

Door entryway recessed
Shorewood (Milwaukee), Wisconsin

Door entryway recessed
Rockford, Illinois

Door entryway recessed
Wisconsin Dells, Wisconsin

Door entryway recessed
Wisconsin Dells, Wisconsin

Door entryway recessed
Wisconsin Dells, Wisconsin

Door entryway recessed
Rockford, Illinois

Door entryway recessed
Independence, Oregon

1.(f.) Entryway Patio:

A porch with no roof provides a paved, extended living area outside the house and it opens the house to the landscape. This results in a great area for those who want full sun. Because there is no roof to limit height, taller items such as tables with umbrellas could be used when creating a sitting area,

Entryway patio
Versailes, Kentucky

After going up the stairs there is an open patio. When approaching the front door, a roof protects it.
Frankfort, Kentucky

Entryway patio
Oak Park, Illinois

91

Entryway patio
Oak Park, Illinois

Entryway patio
Dallas, Oregon

2.(a.) Porch in wall of house:

These porches are carved out living spaces that appear to be rooms with one or two sides open. Depending on the size of the space, this can be more private and offer as much room-like potential as interior rooms.

Porch in wall of house
Bloomington, Illinois

Porch in wall of house
Clinton, Tennessee

Porch in wall of house
Shorewood (Milwaukee), Wisconsin

Porch in wall of house
Evansville, Indiana

Porch in wall of house
Shorewood (Milwaukee), Wisconsin

93

2.(b.) Porch under the roof of the house:

The porches in the following pictures are tucked in under the roof of the house. This porch provides shade for the windows of the house and can provide a deep band of shade at mid-day.

Porch under roof of house
Clinton, Tennessee

Porch under roof of house
Folly Beach, South Carolina

Porch under roof of house
Clinton, Tennessee

Porch under roof of house
Clinton, Tennessee

Porch under roof of house
Clinton, Tennessee

94

At left, top to bottom:

Porch under roof of house
Oak Ridge, Tennessee

Porch under roof of house
Winchester, Kentucky

Porch under roof of house
Winchester, Kentucky

Porch under roof of house
Lexington, Kentucky

Porch under roof of house
Versailes, Kentucky

Porch under roof of house
Georgetown, Kentucky

Porch under roof of house
Danville, Illinois

Porch under roof of house
Evansville, Indiana

Porch under roof of house
Danville, Illinois

Porch under roof of house
Evansville, Indiana

Porch under roof of house
Danville, Illinois

Porch under roof of house
Orfordville, Wisconsin

Porch under roof of house
Orfordville, Wisconsin

Porch under roof of house
Beloit, Wisconsin

Porch under roof of house
Rockford, Illinois

Porch under roof of house
Rockford, Illinois

Porch under roof of house
Rockford, Illinois

Porch under roof of house
Beloit, Wisconsin

Porch under roof of house
Dallas, Oregon

Porch under roof of house
Wisconsin Dells, Wisconsin

Porch under roof of house
Independence, Oregon

Porch under roof of house
Dallas, Oregon

2.(c.) Porch with own roof:

The porch with its own roof appears to be an open room added to the house. This creates a sheltered living space addition to the house that can be enjoyed by the occupants and welcomed visitors.

Porch with own roof
Charleston, South Carolina

Porch with own roof
Savannah, Georgia

Porch with own roof
Ashville, North Carolina

Porch with own roof
Savannah, Georgia

Porch with own roof
Ashville, North Carolina

Porch with own roof
Clinton, Tennessee

Porch with own roof
Winchester, Kentucky

Porch with own roof
Clinton, Tennessee

Porch with own roof
Winchester, Kentucky

Porch with own roof
Oak Ridge, Tennessee

101

Porch with own roof
Winchester, Kentucky

Porch with own roof
Winchester, Kentucky

Porch with own roof
Winchester, Kentucky

Porch with own roof
Winchester, Kentucky

Porch with own roof
Winchester, Kentucky

Porch with own roof
Lexington, Kentucky

Porch with own roof
Lexington, Kentucky

Porch with own roof
Lexington, Kentucky

Porch with own roof
Lexington, Kentucky

Porch with own roof
Lexington, Kentucky

Porch with own roof
Frankfort, Kentucky

Porch with own roof
Versailes, Kentucky

Porch with own roof
Frankfort, Kentucky

Porch with own roof
Versailes, Kentucky

Porch with own roof
Frankfort, Kentucky

Porch with own roof
Georgetown, Kentucky

Porch with own roof
Georgetown, Kentucky

Porch with own roof
Georgetown, Kentucky

Porch with own roof
Evansville, Indiana

Porch with own roof
Evansville, Indiana

Porch with own roof
Princeton, Indiana

Porch with own roof
Evansville, Indiana

Porch with own roof
Bloomington, Illinois

Porch with own roof
Oak Park, Illinois

Porch with own roof
Oak Park, Illinois

Porch with own roof
Oak Park, Illinois

Porch with own roof
Orfordville, Wisconsin

Porch with own roof
Orfordville, Wisconsin

Porch with own roof
Orfordville, Wisconsin

Porch with own roof
Orfordville, Wisconsin

Porch with own roof
Wisconsin Dells, Wisconsin

Porch with own roof
Janesville, Wisconsin

Porch with own roof
Wisconsin Dells, Wisconsin

Porch with own roof
Rockford, Illinois

Porch with own roof
Dallas, Oregon

109

2.(d.) Porch with high entryway:

A colossal way to dramatize the approach to the house is with a grand high entryway. To enhance the affect, the doors and windows under these impressive entryways tend to have extravagant accents.

Porch with high entryway
Charleston, South Carolina

Porch with high entryway
Brownsville, Texas

Porch with high entryway
Charleston, South Carolina

Porch with high entryway
Folly Beach, South Carolina

Porch with high entryway
Clinton, Tennessee

Porch with high entryway
Georgetown, Kentucky

Porch with high entryway
Clinton, Tennessee

Porch with high entryway
Evansville, Indiana

Porch with high entryway
Frankfort, Kentucky

Porch with high entryway
Georgetown, Kentucky

111

Bloomington, Illinois

Porch with high entryway
Bloomington, Illinois

Porch with high entryway
Beloit, Wisconsin

Porch with high entryway
Janesville, Wisconsin

Porch with high entryway
Janesville, Wisconsin

Porch with high entryway
Beloit, Wisconsin

Porch with high entryway
Rockford, Illinois

Porch with high entryway
Dallas, Oregon

Porch with high entryway
Independence, Oregon

Porch with high entryway
Dallas, Oregon

Porch with high entryway
Independence, Oregon

113

2.(e.) Porch with Parapet:
These luxurious porch entryways are made even more dramatic because of the parapet on the top.

Porch with parapet
Savannah, Georgia

Porch with parapet
Charleston, South Carolina

Porch with parapet
Savannah, Georgia

Porch with parapet
Charleston, South Carolina

Porch with parapet
Charleston, South Carolina

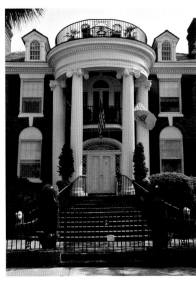

Porch with parapet
Charleston, South Carolina

Porch with parapet
Charleston, South Carolina

Porch with high entryway
Lexington, Kentucky

Porch with parapet
Charleston, South Carolina

Porch with parapet
Ashville, North Carolina

Porch with high entryway
Lexington, Kentucky

Porch with parapet
Lexington, Kentucky

Porch with parapet
Evansville, Indiana

Porch with parapet
Oak Park (Chicago), Illinois

Porch with parapet
Rockord, Illinois

Porch with parapet
Rockford, Illinois

2.(f.) Porch with gable roof:

These pictures have been separated out from the other porches with their own roofs because of the gable roof line. The gable roof gives added height and even more magnitude to the porch.

Porch with gable roof
Beaufort, South Carolina

Porch with gable roof
Charleston, South Carolina

Porch with gable roof
Ashville, North Carolina

Porch with gable roof
Versailes, Kentucky

Porch with gable roof
Ashville, North Carolina

117

Porch with gable roof
Frankfort, Kentucky

Porch with gable roof
Georgetown, Kentucky

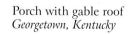

Porch with gable roof
Georgetown, Kentucky

Porch with double gable roof
Georgetown, Kentucky

Porch with gable roof
Georgetown, Kentucky

118

Porch with gable roof
Evansville, Indiana

Porch with gable roof
Georgetown, Kentucky

Porch with gable roof
Princeton, Indiana

Porch with gable roof
Bloomington, Illinois

Porch with gable roof
Bloomington, Illinois

Porch with gable roof
Bloomington, Illinois

Porch with gable roof
Beloit, Wisconsin

Porch with gable roof
Rockford, Illinois

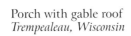

Porch with gable roof
Trempealeau, Wisconsin

Porch with gable roof
Rockford, Illinois

Porch with gable roof
Dallas, Oregon

Porch with gable roof
Independence, Oregon

Porch with gable roof
Dallas, Oregon

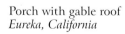

Porch with gable roof
Independence, Oregon

Porch with gable roof
Eureka, California

2.(g.) Ground floor porch with upper porch:

One concept that's better than one porch is two porches—one above the other. With twin porches the house becomes extended beyond the actual walls of the house. The porches add outdoor living space to all the adjacent interior rooms on both floors.

Porch with upper porch
Beaufort, South Carolina

Porch with upper porch
Savannah, Georgia

Porch with upper porch
Charleston, South Carolina

123

Porch with upper porch
Hendersonville, North Carolina

Porch with upper porch
Evansville, Indiana

Porch with upper porch
Winchester, Kentucky

Porch with upper porch
Georgetown, Kentucky

124

Porch with upper porch
South Beloit, Illinois

Porch with upper porch
Monmouth, Oregon

Porch with upper porch
Dallas, Oregon

Porch with upper porch
Orfordville, Wisconsin

A pergola is a great way to introduce a covered walkway into an area where people may want to relax, enjoy a meal or walk in the shade on a hot day.
Orlando, Florida

This pergola is in a shopping area.
Orlando, Florida

Pergolas often appear in garden areas and are used as support structures for vines.
Brookgreen Gardens, South Carolina

3. Pergola in the entryway:

Pergolas that often appear in gardens and the private seating areas at the rear and sides of the house are also used at the front of the house. They enhance the entryway, shade the walkway and entryway, and create another living area at the front of the house.

A grand entryway is created with this sturdy pergola over the walkway at the entrance to the house.
Georgetown, South Carolina

Entryway with Pergola
Charleston, South Carolina

A pergola stands alone in the rear area of the property.
Chattanooga, Tennessee

126

The pergola has been added to the side of the house giving the appearance of extending the porch and the house.
Clinton, Tennessee

Entryway with Pergola
Lexington, Kentucky

Entryway with Pergola
Dallas, Oregon

127

Entryway with Pergola
San Diego, California

Entryway with Pergola
San Diego, California

Entryway with Pergola
San Diego, California

Entryway with Pergola
San Diego, California

Entryway with Pergola
San Diego, California

Entryway with Pergola
San Diego, California

Entryway with Pergola
San Diego, California

Chapter IV. Entryway with Stairway

Entryway with stairway
Savannah, Georgia

A stairway is usually installed because it is a necessity, but on occasion stairways are added to create dimension and interest to the entryway. Either way designs can be varied and exotic. Stairways combine style and functionality. Each stairway creates its own imprint on the overall appearance of the entryway. Handicap walkways fall into much the same category.

There are many styles of stairways: single and double, straight or converging, one or a series of flights, narrow or wide, curved, spiral or straight, deep or shallow steps, low or high steps, and bordered by railings, balustrades, or walls. Another thing to watch for in the pictures is the material used to create the stairways. Exterior stairs must be stable, slip resistant, and non-combustible. Material choices depend on aesthetics, cost, maintenance needs, and climate. An entry stairway that handles all up-and-down foot traffic and is in a highly visible location is bound to be much more grand than a stairway to a hardly-ever-used area.

Entryway with stairway
Laredo, Texas

Entryway with stairway
Savannah, Georgia

Entryway with stairway
Savannah, Georgia

Entryway with stairway
Savannah, Georgia

Entryway with stairway
Savannah, Georgia

Entryway with stairway
Savannah, Georgia

Entryway with stairway
Savannah, Georgia

Entryway with stairway
Savannah, Georgia

Entryway with stairway
Savannah, Georgia

Entryway with stairway
Hilton Head, South Carolina

Entryway with stairway
Savannah, Georgia

Entryway with stairway
Hilton Head, South Carolina

Entryway with stairway
Hilton Head, South Carolina

Entryway with stairway – Notice
the location of the palm tree.
Hilton Head, South Carolina

Entryway with stairway
Hilton Head, South Carolina

133

Entryway with stairway
Hilton Head, South Carolina

Entryway with stairway
Hilton Head, South Carolina

Entryway with stairway
Hilton Head, South Carolina

Entryway with stairway
Hilton Head, South Carolina

Entryway with stairway
Hilton Head, South Carolina

Entryway with stairway
Hilton Head, South Carolina

Entryway with stairway
Beaufort, South Carolina

135

Entryway with stairway
Beaufort, South Carolina

Entryway with stairway
Beaufort, South Carolina

Entryway with stairway
Beaufort, South Carolina

Entryway with stairway
Beaufort, South Carolina

Entryway with stairway
Beaufort, South Carolina

Entryway with stairway
Charleston, South Carolina

Entryway with stairway
Beaufort, South Carolina

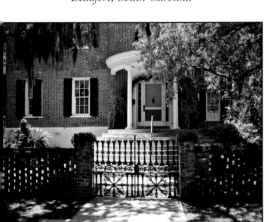

Entryway with stairway
Charleston, South Carolina

Entryway with stairway
Beaufort, South Carolina

137

Entryway with stairway
Charleston, South Carolina

Entryway with stairway
Charleston, South Carolina

Entryway with stairway
Charleston, South Carolina

Entryway with stairway
Charleston, South Carolina

Entryway with stairway
Charleston,
South Carolina

Entryway with stairway
Folly Beach, South Carolina

Entryway with stairway
Charleston, South Carolina

Entryway with stairway
Charleston, South Carolina

Entryway with stairway
Folly Beach, South Carolina

Entryway with stairway
Folly Beach, South Carolina

Entryway with
stairway
*Folly Beach, South
Carolina*

Entryway with stairway
Folly Beach, South Carolina

Entryway with stairway
Folly Beach, South Carolina

Entryway with stairway
Folly Beach, South Carolina

Entryway with stairway
Folly Beach, South Carolina

141

Entryway with stairway
Folly Beach, South Carolina

Entryway with stairway
Folly Beach, South Carolina

Entryway with stairway
Folly Beach, South Carolina

Entryway with stairway
Folly Beach, South Carolina

Entryway with stairway
Folly Beach, South Carolina

Entryway with stairway
Folly Beach, South Carolina

Entryway with stairway
Folly Beach, South Carolina

Entryway with stairway
Folly Beach, South Carolina

Entryway with stairway
Folly Beach, South Carolina

Entryway with stairway
Folly Beach, South Carolina

Entryway with stairway
Folly Beach, South Carolina

Entryway with stairway
Charleston, South Carolina

Entryway with stairway
Charleston, South Carolina

Entryway with stairway
Folly Beach, South Carolina

Entryway with stairway
Charleston, South Carolina

Entryway with stairway
Charleston, South Carolina

Entryway with stairway
Charleston, South Carolina

Entryway with stairway
Charleston, South Carolina

Entryway with stairway
Charleston, South Carolina

Entryway with stairway
Charleston, South Carolina

Entryway with stairway
Charleston, South Carolina

Entryway
with stairway
*Charleston,
South Carolina*

Entryway with stairway. Don't miss the surround on the doorway.
Charleston, South Carolina

Entryway with stairway
Charleston, South Carolina

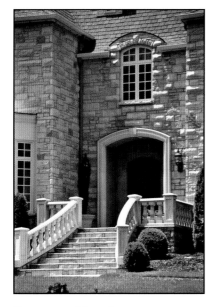

Entryway with stairway
Hendersonville, North Carolina

Entryway with stairway
Ashville, North Carolina

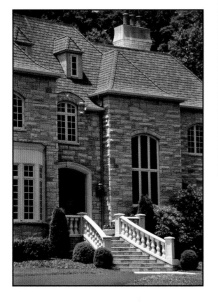

Entryway with stairway
Clinton, Tennessee

Entryway with stairway
Clinton, Tennessee

Entryway with stairway
Oak Ridge, Tennessee

Entryway with stairway
Lexington, Kentucky

Entryway with stairway
Winchester, Kentucky

Entryway with stairway
Frankfort, Kentucky

Entryway with stairway
Lexington, Kentucky

Entryway with stairway
Frankfort, Kentucky

Entryway with stairway
Frankfort, Kentucky

Entryway with stairway
Evansville, Indiana

Entryway with stairway
Frankfort, Kentucky

Entryway with stairway
Orfordville, Wisconsin

Entryway with stairway
Orfordville, Wisconsin

Entryway with stairway
Rockford, Illinois

Entryway with stairway
Shorewood (Milwaukee), Wisconsin

Entryway with stairway
Rockford, Illinois

Entryway with stairway
Rockford, Illinois

Entryway with stairway
San Diego, California

Entryway with stairway
San Diego, California

Entryway with stairway
San Diego, California

Chapter V. Walkways and Driveways

Walkways, driveways, and sidewalks can provide much-needed curb appeal to homes. They are fast becoming a point of artistic expression by way of a multitude of decorative options. While plain gray concrete is still the most often walkway installed, there are numerous alternatives. If you already have a walkway, there are plenty of ways you can make it unique. From concrete engraving, to concrete overlays, to saw-cut patterns, to random cut patterns. A simple walkway can be turned into an elegant approach with the use of curves, patterns, and different materials.

Driveway paving materials fall into two main categories: solid-surface (i.e., smooth, seamless, even surfaces) and aggregate-surface. The most popular options lie in the first category, led by asphalt and concrete. Aggregate-surface driveway paving materials include gravel and crushed stone. Driveway pavers lie in between these two main categories.

The walkways and driveways shown here are the results of the efforts made by homeowners who wanted to improve their entryways. In some cases the results may be the combined efforts of separate installations made over time by different occupants. The walkway and driveway improvements have a dramatic affect on the overall appearance of the entryways.

Walkway/Driveway
Kansas City

Walkway/Driveway
Pearsall, Texas

Walkway/Driveway
McAllen, Texas

Walkway/Driveway
Mission, Texas

Walkway/Driveway
Beaufort, South Carolina

Walkway/Driveway
Indian Wells, Texas

153

Walkway/Driveway
Beaufort, South Carolina

Walkway/Driveway
Jacksonville, Florida

Walkway/Driveway
Florida Keys

Walkway/Driveway
Atlanta, Georgia

154

Walkway/Driveway

Walkway/Driveway

Walkway/Driveway
Savannah, Georgia

Walkway/Driveway

Walkway/Driveway

Walkway/Driveway
*Folly Beach, Swouth
Carolina*

156

Walkway/Driveway
Folly Beach, South Carolina

Walkway/Driveway
Charleston, South Carolina

Walkway/Driveway
Charleston, South Carolina

Walkway/Driveway
Charleston, South Carolina

Walkway/Driveway
Charleston, South Carolina

Walkway/Driveway
Charleston, South Carolina

Walkway/Driveway
Charleston, South Carolina

Walkway/Driveway
Charleston, South Carolina

Walkway/Driveway
Charleston, South Carolina

Walkway/Driveway
Charleston, South Carolina

Walkway/Driveway
Charleston, South Carolina

Walkway/Driveway
Charleston, South Carolina

159

Walkway/Driveway
Charleston, South Carolina

Walkway/Driveway
Charleston, South Carolina

Walkway/Driveway
Charleston, South Carolina

Walkway/Driveway
Charleston, South Carolina

160

Walkway/Driveway
Charleston, South Carolina

Walkway/Driveway
Charleston, South Carolina

Walkway/Driveway
Charleston, South Carolina

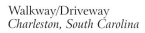

Walkway/Driveway
Charleston, South Carolina

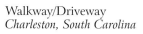

Walkway/Driveway
Charleston, South Carolina

Walkway/Driveway
Charleston, South Carolina

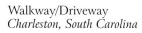

Walkway/Driveway
Charleston, South Carolina

Walkway/Driveway
Charleston, South Carolina

Walkway/Driveway
Charleston, South Carolina

Walkway/Driveway
Charleston, South Carolina

Walkway/Driveway
Charleston, South Carolina

Walkway/Driveway
Charleston, South Carolina

Walkway/Driveway
Charleston, South Carolina

Walkway/Driveway
Charleston, South Carolina

Walkway/Driveway
Charleston, South Carolina

Walkway/Driveway
Charleston, South Carolina

Walkway/Driveway
Charleston, South Carolina

Walkway/Driveway
Charleston, South Carolina

Walkway/Driveway
Charleston, South Carolina

Walkway/
Driveway
*Charleston,
South Carolina*

165

Walkway/Driveway
Charleston, South Carolina

Walkway/Driveway
Charleston, South Carolina

Walkway/Driveway
Charleston, South Carolina

Walkway/Driveway
Charleston, South Carolina

166

Walkway/Driveway
Charleston, South Carolina

Walkway/Driveway
Charleston, South Carolina

Walkway/Driveway
Charleston, South Carolina

Walkway/Driveway
Charleston, South Carolina

Walkway/Driveway
*Charleston, South
Carolina*

Walkway/Driveway
Charleston, South Carolina

Walkway/Driveway
Charleston, South Carolina

168

Walkway/Driveway
Charleston, South Carolina

Walkway/Driveway
Charleston, South Carolina

Walkway/Driveway
Charleston, South Carolina

Walkway/Driveway
Charleston, South Carolina

Walkway/Driveway
Charleston, South Carolina

169

Walkway/Driveway
Charleston, South Carolina

Walkway/Driveway
Hendersonville, North Carolina

Walkway/Driveway
Ashville, North Carolina

Walkway/Driveway
Ashville, North Carolina

Walkway/Driveway
Ashville, North Carolina

170

Walkway/Driveway
Clinton, Tennessee

Walkway/Driveway
Clinton, Tennessee

Walkway/Driveway
Winchester, Kentucky

Walkway/Driveway
Winchester, Kentucky

Walkway/Driveway
Winchester, Kentucky

171

Walkway/Driveway
Winchester, Kentucky

Walkway/Driveway
Winchester, Kentucky

Walkway/Driveway
Winchester, Kentucky

Walkway/Driveway
Winchester, Kentucky

Walkway/Driveway
Lexington, Kentucky

Walkway/Driveway
Versailes, Kentucky

Walkway/Driveway
Frankfort, Kentucky

Walkway/Driveway
Frankfort, Kentucky

Walkway/Driveway
Frankfort, Kentucky

Walkway/Driveway
Frankfort, Kentucky

Walkway/Driveway
Lexington, Kentucky

Walkway/Driveway
Lexington, Kentucky

174

Walkway/Driveway
Lexington, Kentucky

Walkway/Driveway
Frankfort, Kentucky

Walkway/Driveway
Frankfort, Kentucky

175

Walkway/Driveway
Frankfort, Kentucky

Walkway/Driveway
Frankfort, Kentucky

Walkway/Driveway
Frankfort, Kentucky

Walkway/Driveway
Frankfort, Kentucky

Walkway/Driveway
Frankfort, Kentucky

177

Walkway/Driveway
Frankfort, Kentucky

Walkway/Driveway
Frankfort, Kentucky

Walkway/Driveway
Georgetown, Kentucky

Walkway/Driveway
Georgetown, Kentucky

Walkway/Driveway
Georgetown, Kentucky

Walkway/Driveway
Georgetown, Kentucky

Walkway/Driveway
Georgetown, Kentucky

Walkway/Driveway
Evansville, Indiana

Walkway/Driveway
Georgetown, Kentucky

Walkway/Driveway
Bloomington, Illinois

Walkway/Driveway
Oak Park, Illinois

Walkway/Driveway
Orfordville, Wisconsin

Walkway/Driveway
Beloit, Wisconsin

Walkway/Driveway
Beloit, Wisconsin

Walkway/Driveway
Beloit, Wisconsin

Walkway/Driveway
Shorewood (Milwaukee),
Wisconsin

Walkway/Driveway
Shorewood (Milwaukee), Wisconsin

Walkway/Driveway
Shorewood (Milwaukee), Wisconsin

Walkway/Driveway
Shorewood (Milwaukee), Wisconsin

183

Walkway/Driveway
Shorewood (Milwaukee), Wisconsin

Walkway/Driveway
Franklin (Milwaukee), Wisconsin

Walkway/Driveway
Franklin (Milwaukee), Wisconsin

Walkway/Driveway
Franklin (Milwaukee), Wisconsin

Walkway/Driveway
Lake Geneva, Wisconsin

Walkway/Driveway
Lake Geneva, Wisconsin

Walkway/Driveway
Rockford, Illinois

Walkway/Driveway
Rockford, Illinois

Walkway/Driveway
Rockford, Illinois

Walkway/Driveway
Wisconsin Dells, Wisconsin

186

Walkway/Driveway
Wisconsin Dells, Wisconsin

Walkway/Driveway
Wisconsin Dells, Wisconsin

Walkway/Driveway
Wisconsin Dells, Wisconsin

Walkway/Driveway
Dallas, Oregon

Walkway/Driveway
Wisconsin Dells, Wisconsin

Walkway/Driveway
Dallas, Oregon

Walkway/Driveway
Dallas, Oregon

Walkway/Driveway
Dallas, Oregon

Walkway/Driveway
Dallas, Oregon

Walkway/Driveway
Monmouth, Oregon

Walkway/Driveway
Independence, Oregon

Walkway/Driveway
San Diego, California

Walkway/Driveway
San Diego, California

Chapter VI. Glossary

Alcove – a recessed space.

Arabesque – a complex, ornate design of intertwined floral, foliate, and geometric figures.

Arbor – a latticework bower intertwined with climbing vines and flowers.

Art glass – stained, etched or engraved glass.

> www.sperlich.com/www.auroraglass.com/glossary.html
> sdglassart.com/index.html

Balustrade – a railing at the side of a staircase or balcony to prevent people from falling

> www.thecanterastonesource.com/balustrades.htm

Bower – a shaded, leafy recess; an arbor.

Brackets – any of a series of fancifully shaped false consoles beneath a cornice.

> www.cumberlandwoodcraft.com/corbels-and-brackets.htm
> www.imperialdesign.on.ca/ELEMENTS/ALL-CORBELS/ corbel-mix.htm

Broken pediment – a pediment open or broken at the apex, base or both, and the gap often filled with an urn, acorn, or other ornament. (See pediment)

Caming – the metal banding that joins panels of glass together in a design

Capital – *Architecture* – the distinctively treated upper end of a column.

Column – a supporting pillar consisting of a base, a cylindrical shaft, and a capital.

Console – An often scroll-shaped bracket used for decoration or for supporting a projecting member, such as a cornice or shelf.

Converging stairs – incline toward each other, as lines that are not parallel.

Corbels – a bracket of stone, wood, brick, or other building material, projecting from the face of a wall and generally used to support a cornice or arch.

> www.cumberlandwoodcraft.com/corbels-and-brackets.htm
> www.architecturaldepot.com/c/corbels/?source=google&ke yword=corbels

Cornice – any prominent, continuous, horizontally projecting feature surmounting a wall or other construction, or dividing it horizontally for compositional purposes.

Doorframe – the frame of a doorway, including two jambs and a lintel, or head.

Doorknocker – a device (usually metal and ornamental) attached by a hinge to a door.

Door surrounds – arch surrounding the whole door, an arch halfway around the door, or even just at the top of the door.
www.thecanterastonesource.com/entryways-1.htm

Door topper – Door Topper tops a door or window.
www.saladotex.com/WALL_TAPESTRY_TOPPERS_RODS_HARDWARE.html
www.corallight.com/shop.cfm?tgt=dept&DID=8

Entryway – the doorway and area leading up to it that makes up the outside entrance to your home.

Gable roof – a roof sloping downward in two parts at an angle from a central ridge, so as to leave a gable at each end. Also called pitched roof.

Geometric pattern – resembling or employing the simple rectilinear or curvilinear lines or figures used in geometry.

Ionic columns – Greek columns identified by the scroll-shaped ornaments at the capital, which resemble a ram's horns. The Ionic column rests on a rounded base.

Landing – the floor at the head of a flight of stairs.

Pane – a framed section of a window or door that is usually filled with a sheet of glass or other transparent material.

Parapet – a low railing or wall to protect the edge of a platform, roof, or bridge.

Paved – to cover or lay (a road, walk, etc.) with concrete, stones, bricks, tiles, wood, or the like, so as to make a firm, level surface.

Pediment – a triangular element, similar to or derivative of a Grecian pediment, used widely in architecture and decoration. (See broken pediment)

Pergola – an arbor formed of horizontal trelliswork supported on columns or posts

Pineapple sculptures – The classic symbol of hospitality.
www.winterthurgifts.com/product.cfm/mc/2/ct/15/sid/2069

Patio – an area, usually paved, adjoining a house and used as an area for outdoor lounging, dining, etc.
www.concretenetwork.com/concrete/concrete_patio/?p=Patios

Porch – a structure attached to the exterior of a building, often forming a covered entrance. A covered platform, usually having a separate roof, located at an entrance to a building.
www.hgtv.com/hgtv/dc_design_porch_sunroom/0,1792,HGTV_3380,00.html

Railings – a fencelike barrier composed of one or more horizontal rails supported by widely spaced uprights (balustrade).
http://www.backyardamerica.com/deck_railings.htm

Sculptured – the art of carving, modeling, welding, or otherwise producing figurative or abstract works of art in three dimensions, as in relief, intaglio, or in the round.

Sidelights – a fixed or utilitarian framed glass alongside a door or window opening

Sidewalk – a walk, esp. a paved one, at the side of a street or road.

Stairs, a way of access (upward and downward) consisting of a set of steps

Stairway – a series or flight of steps.
> http://archrecord.construction.com/resources/conteduc/archives/research/6_00_1.asp

Steps – a support for the foot in ascending or descending.

Stock of photography – consists of existing photographs that can be licensed for specific uses.

Stoop – a small raised platform, approached by steps and sometimes having a roof and seats, at the entrance of a house.

Strawberry pot – strawberry pots are the pots that are shaped like an urn and have "pockets" up and down the sides. They are made especially for growing strawberries and you can also grow herbs, flowers or other plants in them.
> www.rainyside.com/container/YeOldStrawberryPot.html

Surrounds – arch surrounding the whole door, an arch halfway around the door, or even just at the top of the door.
> http://www.thecanterastonesource.com/entryways-1.htm

Topiary – sculptured greenery
> http://www.homedecorators.com/Home_Decor/Home_Accents/Topiaries/

Topper – a door crown that adds a special touch to that hard to decorate area above the doorway.

Transom – a window (can be hinged) above a door or another window.

Urn – a large or decorative vase, esp. one with an ornamental foot or pedestal.
> www.nextag.com/planter-urn/search-html
> http://hpotter.com/index.php?main_page=index&cPath=1_20

Walkway – the walk of a house, leading from the door to the sidewalk or road.